Adult Coloring Book:

Animals Coloring Pages for Stress Relieve, Calming and Stay Focus

James D Glover

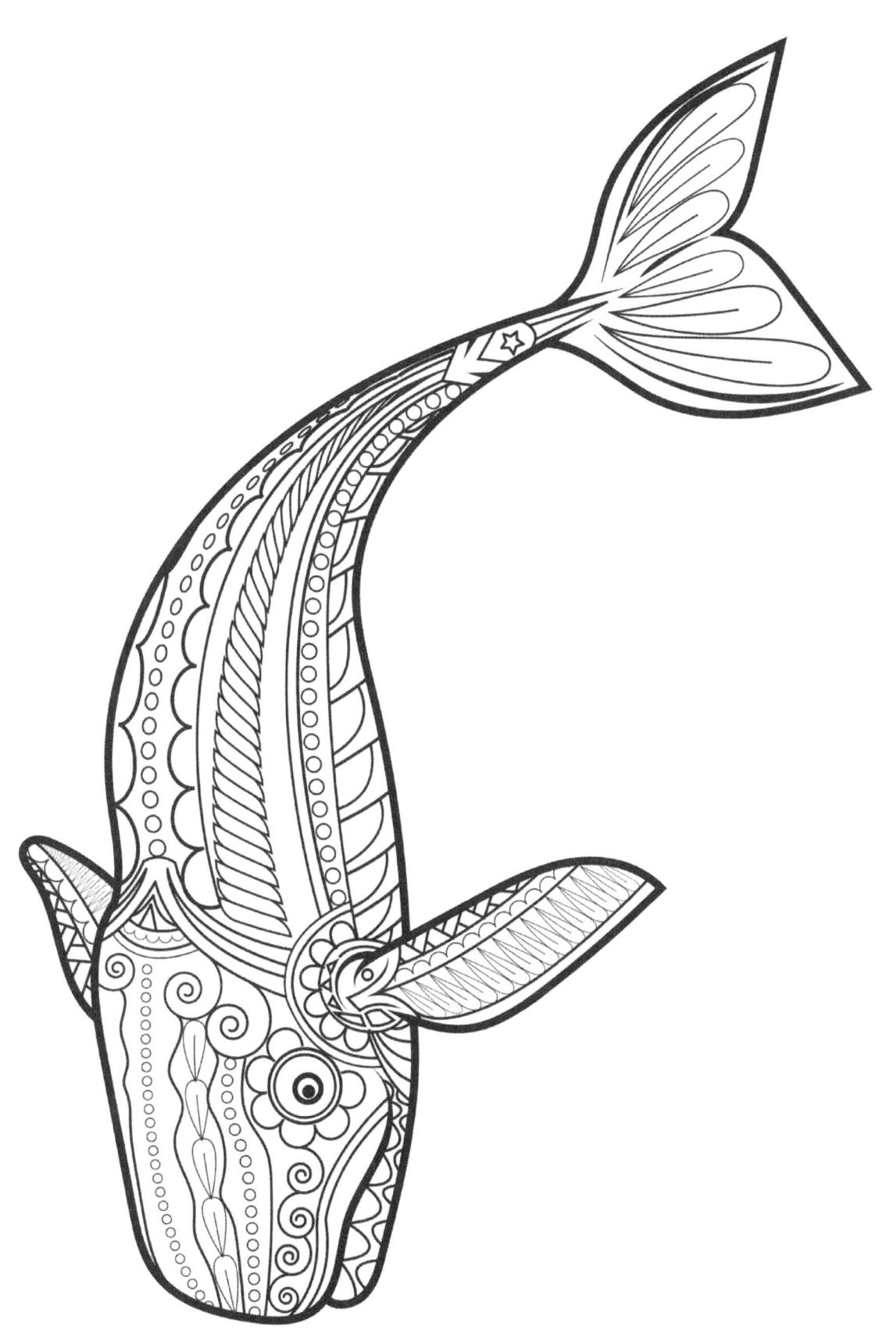

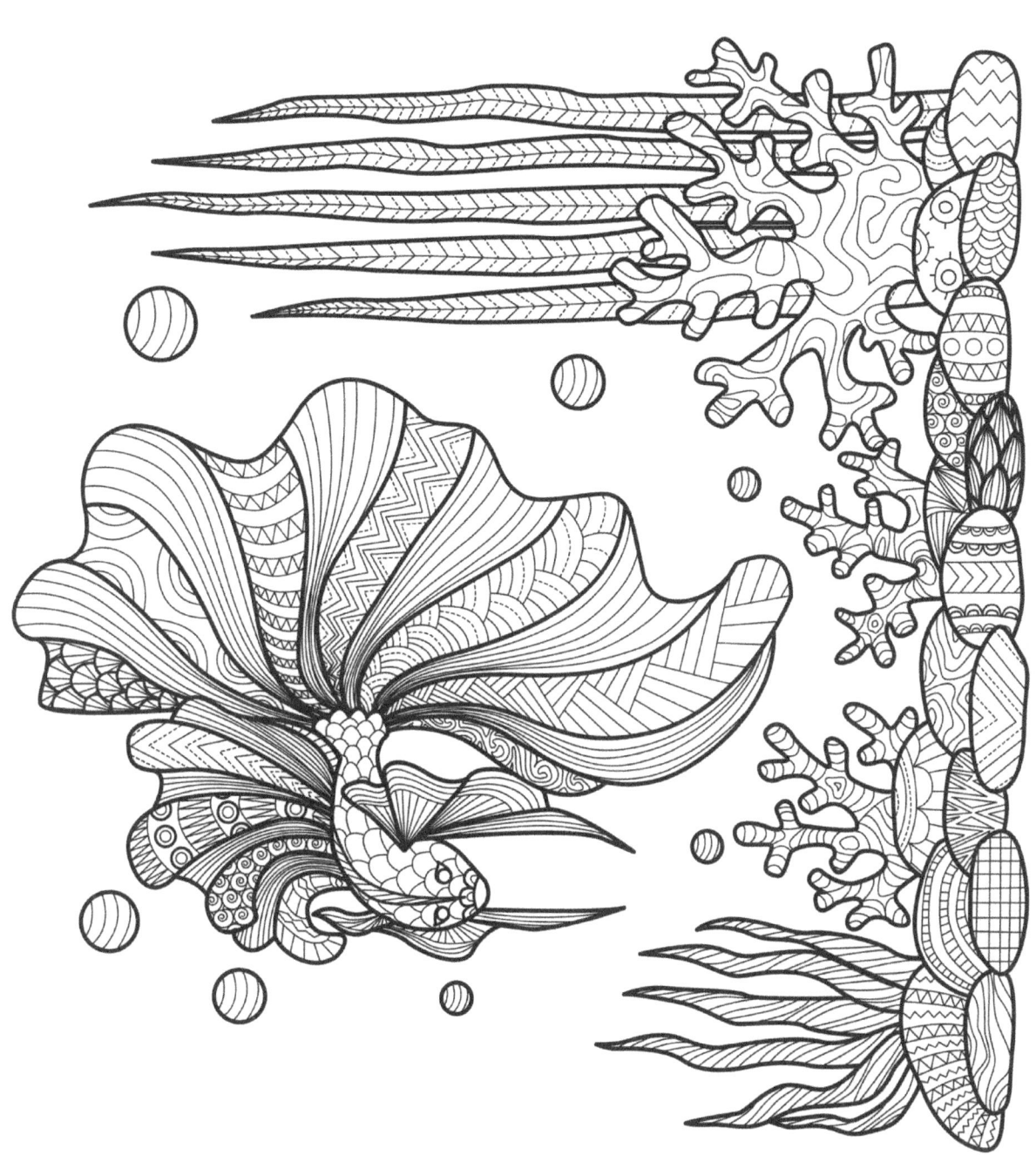

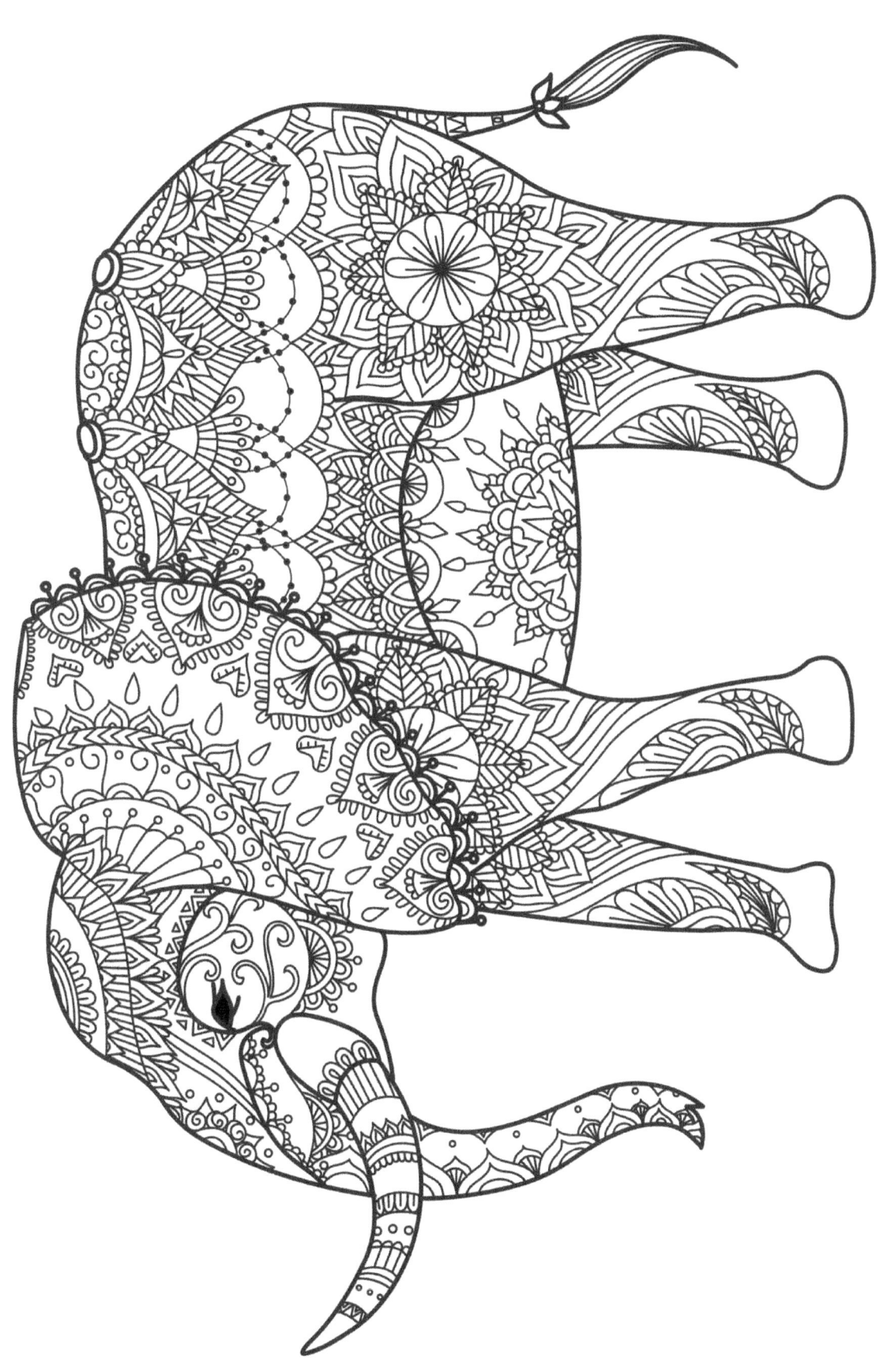

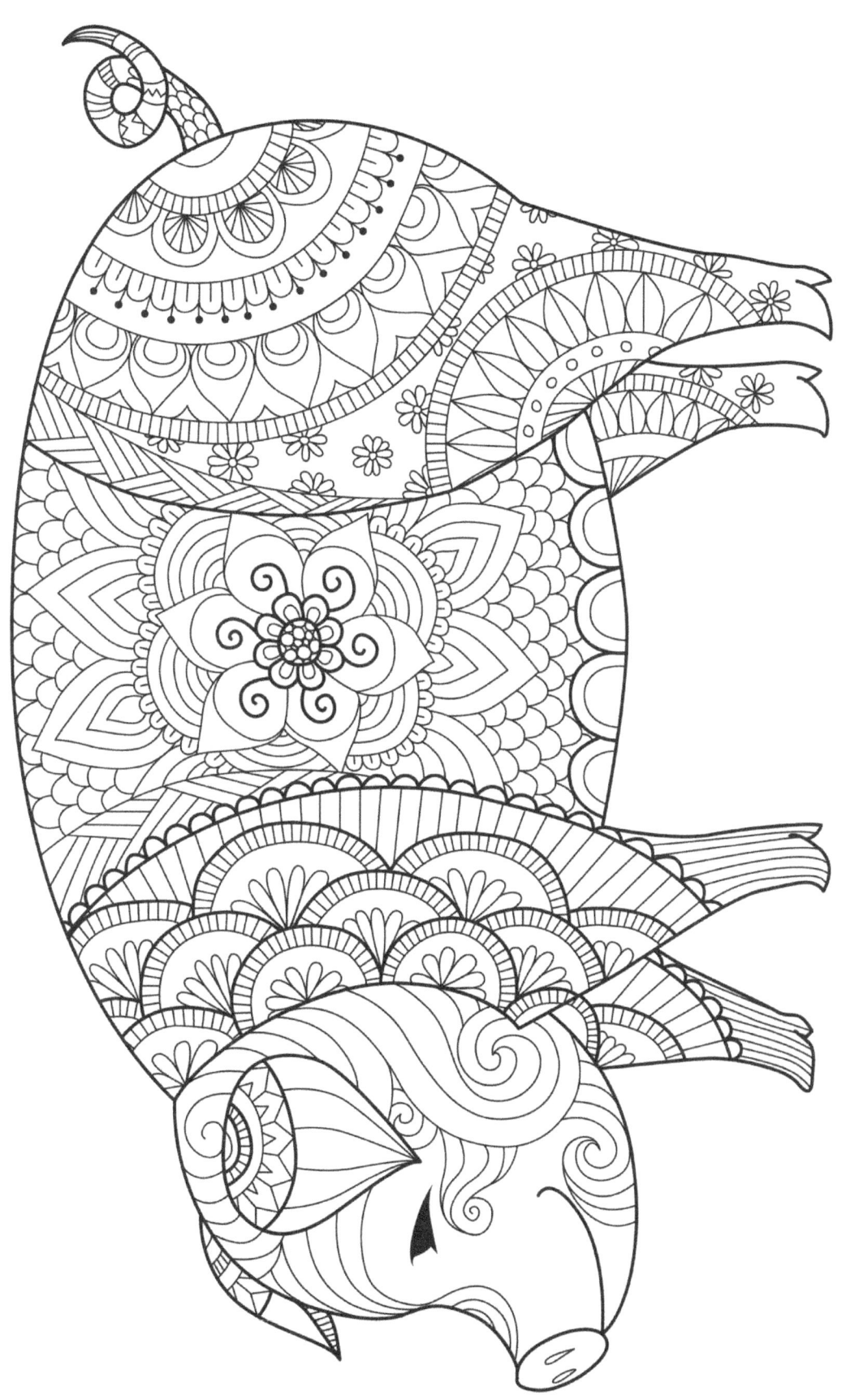

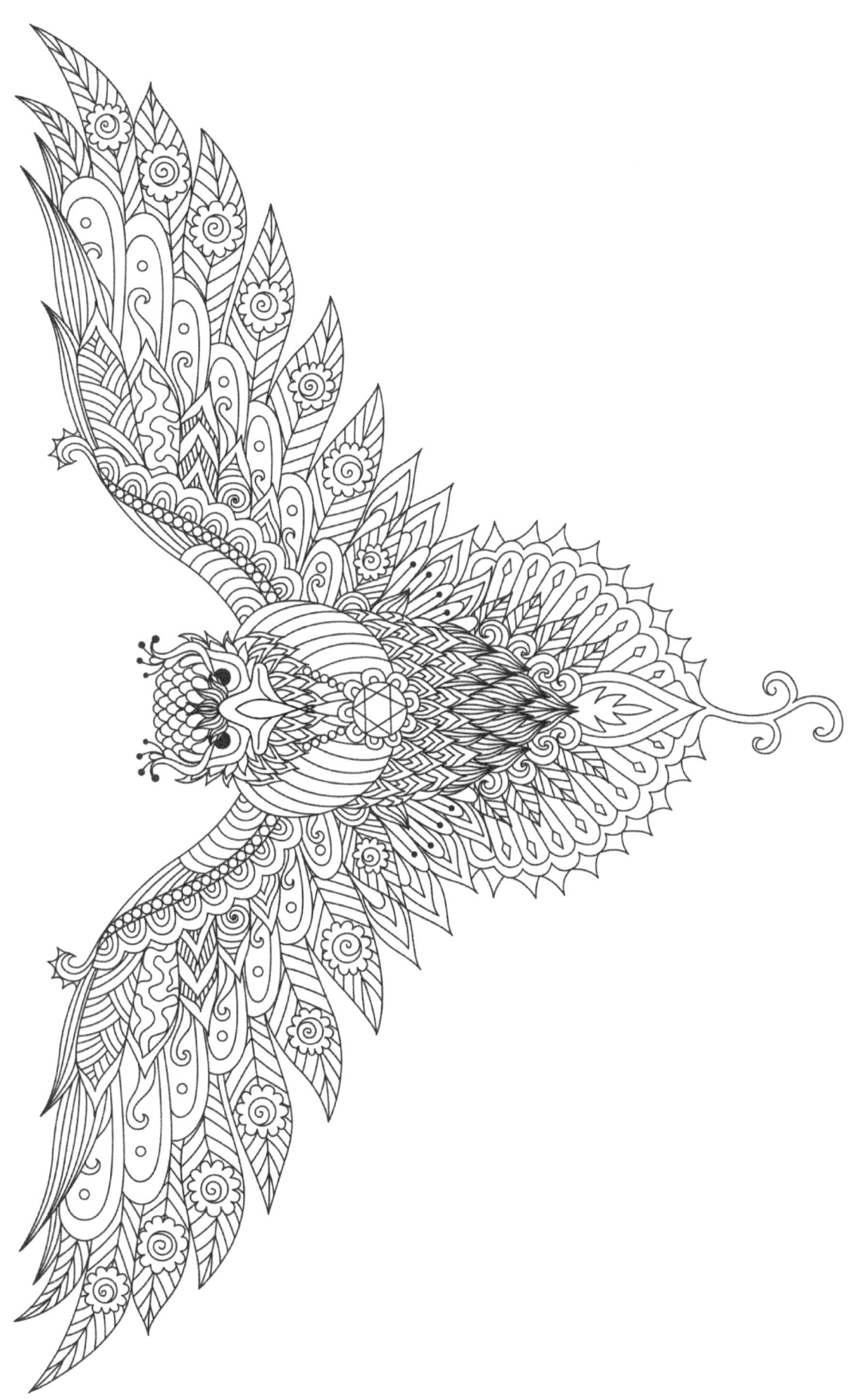

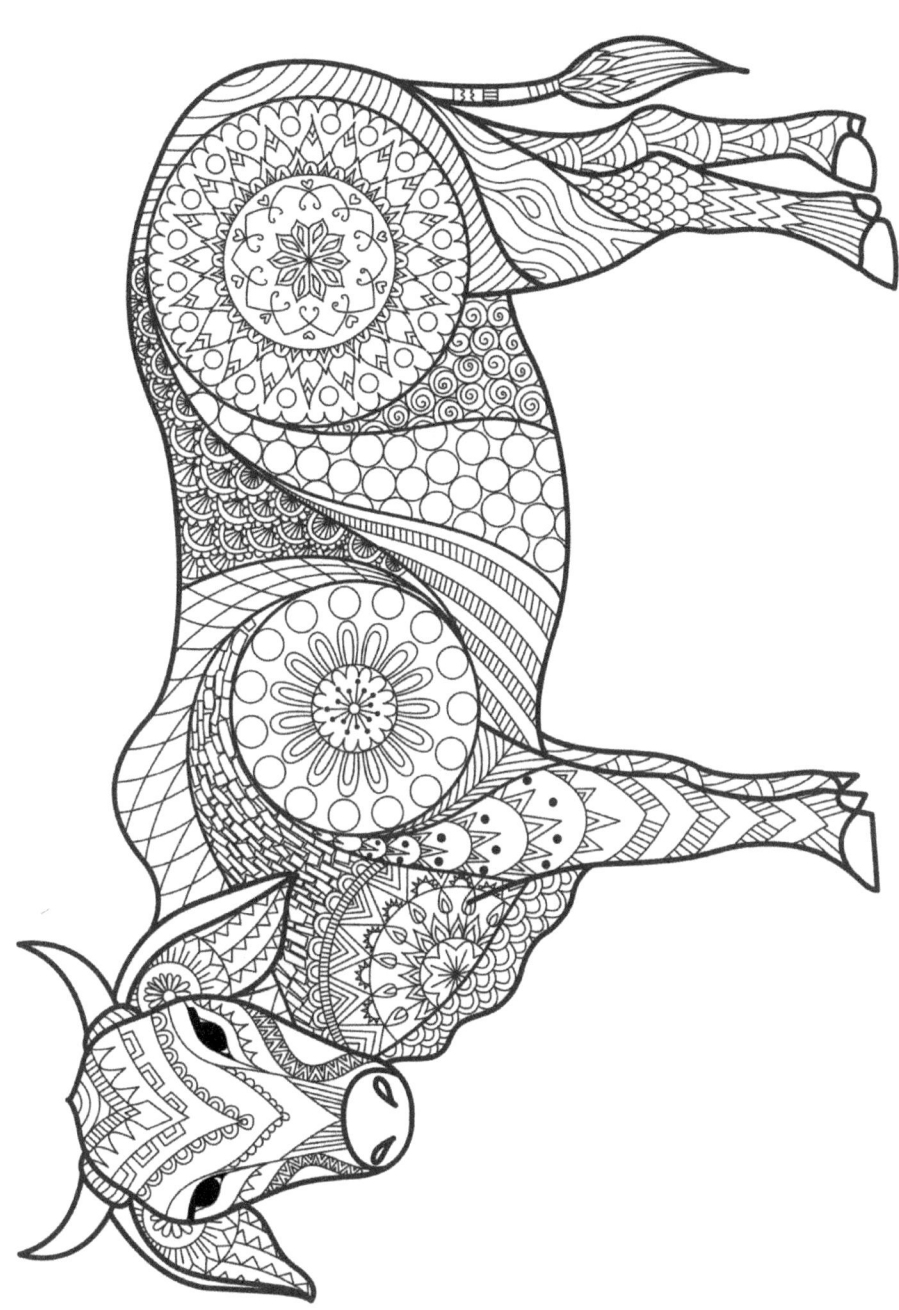

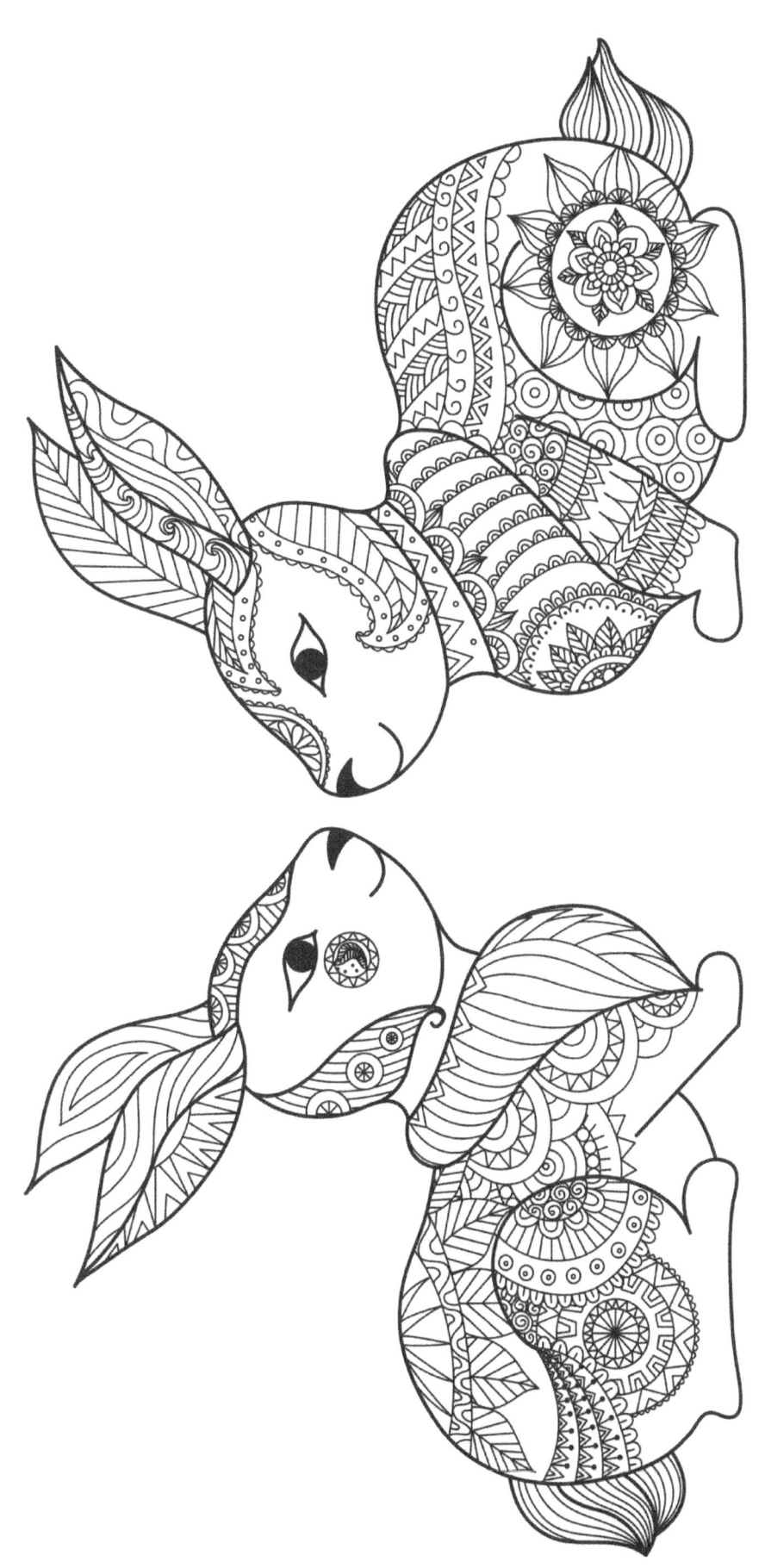

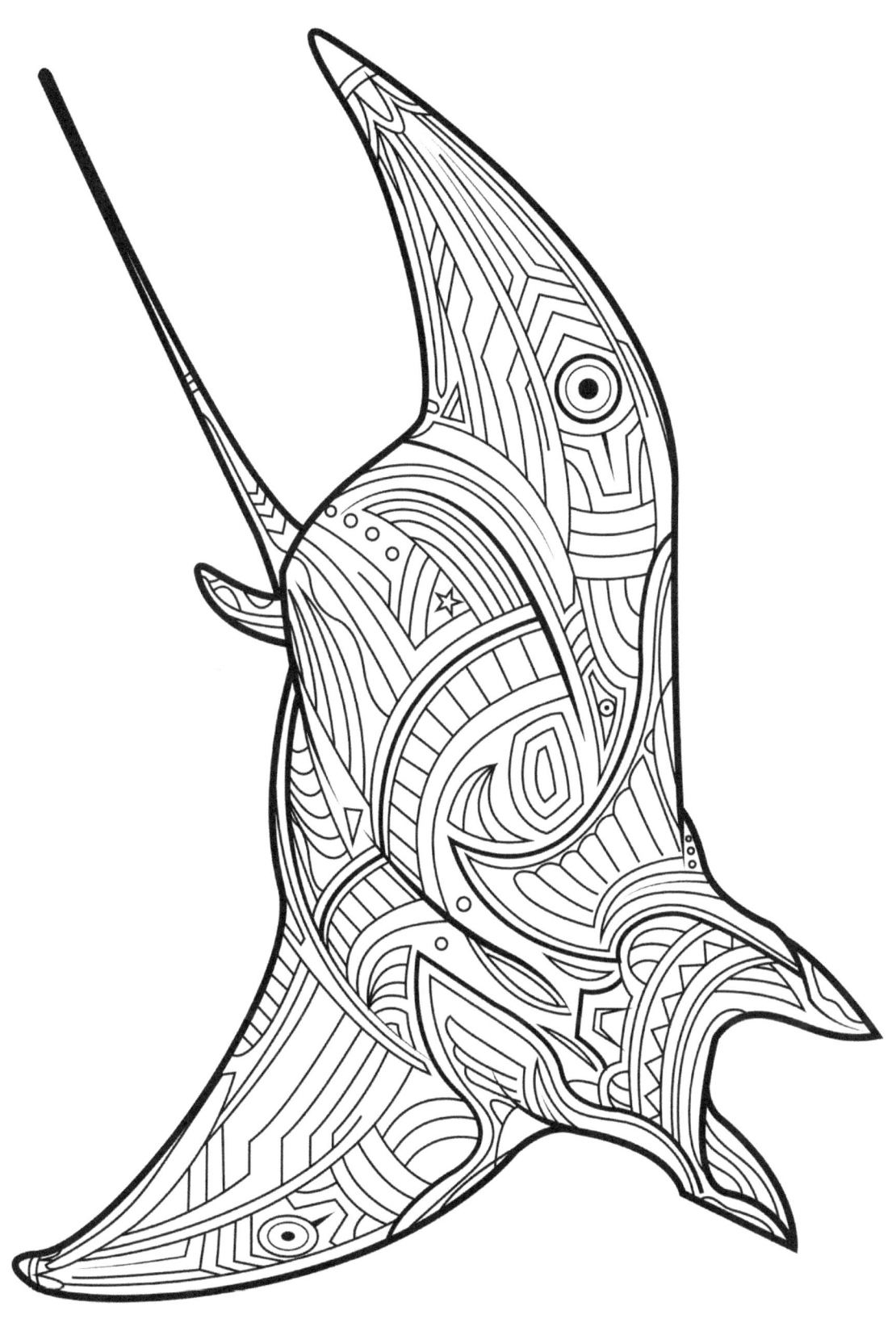

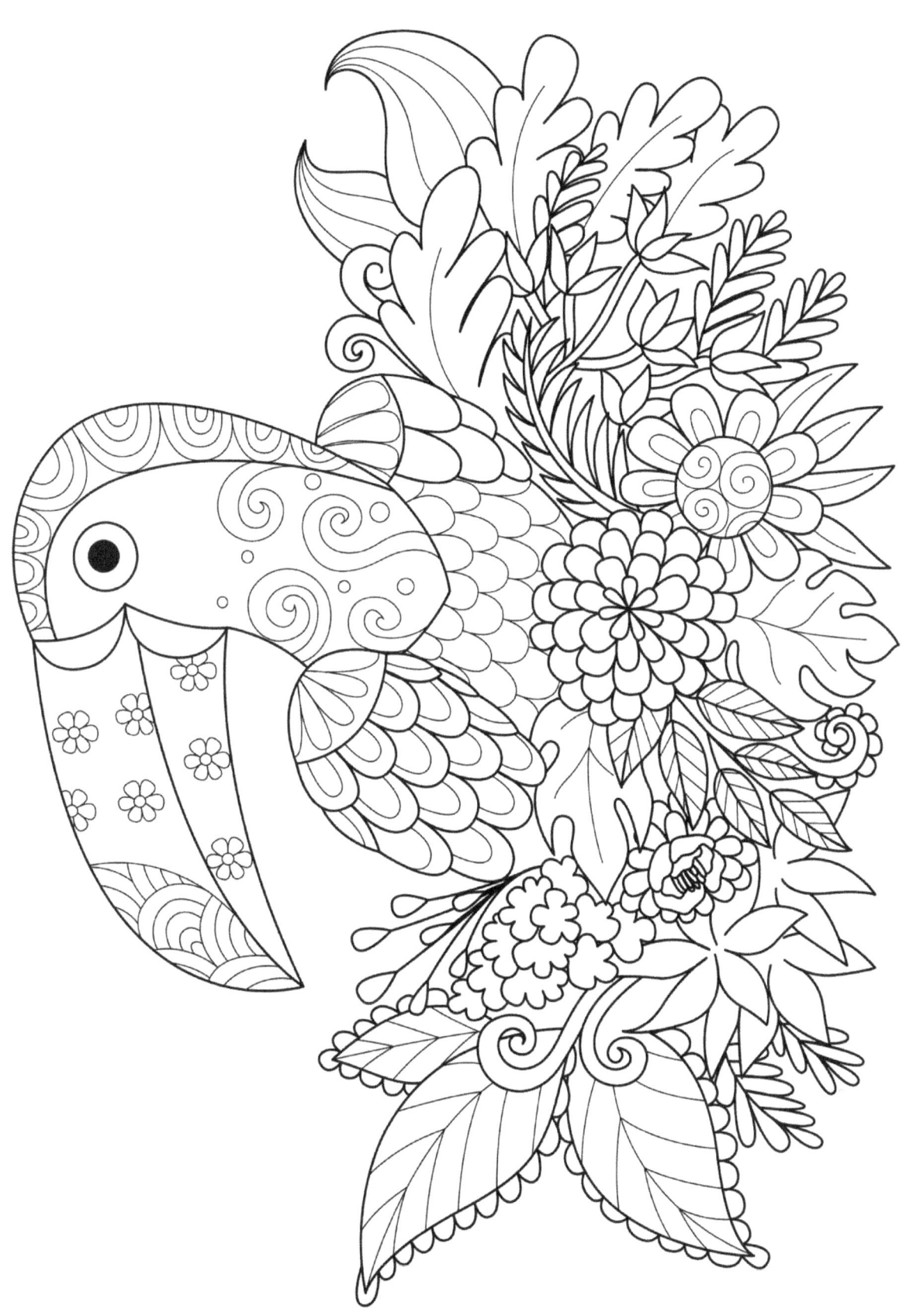

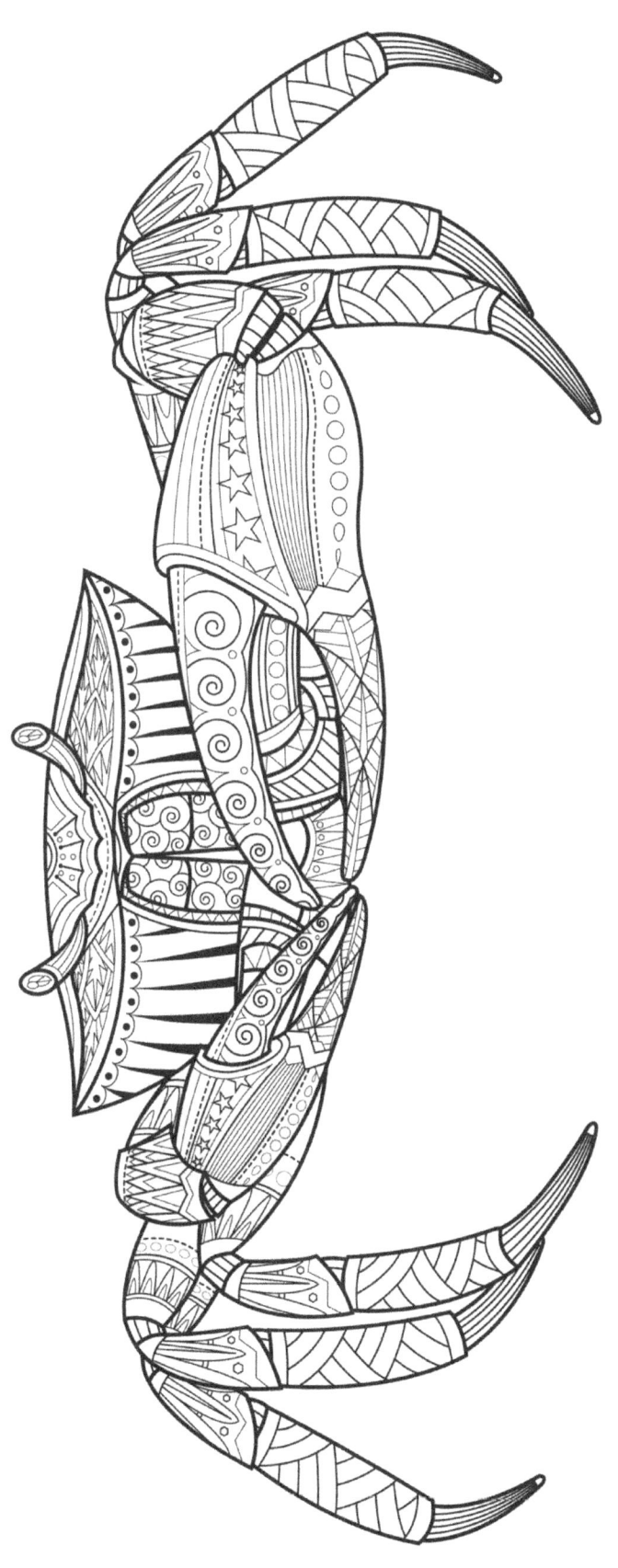

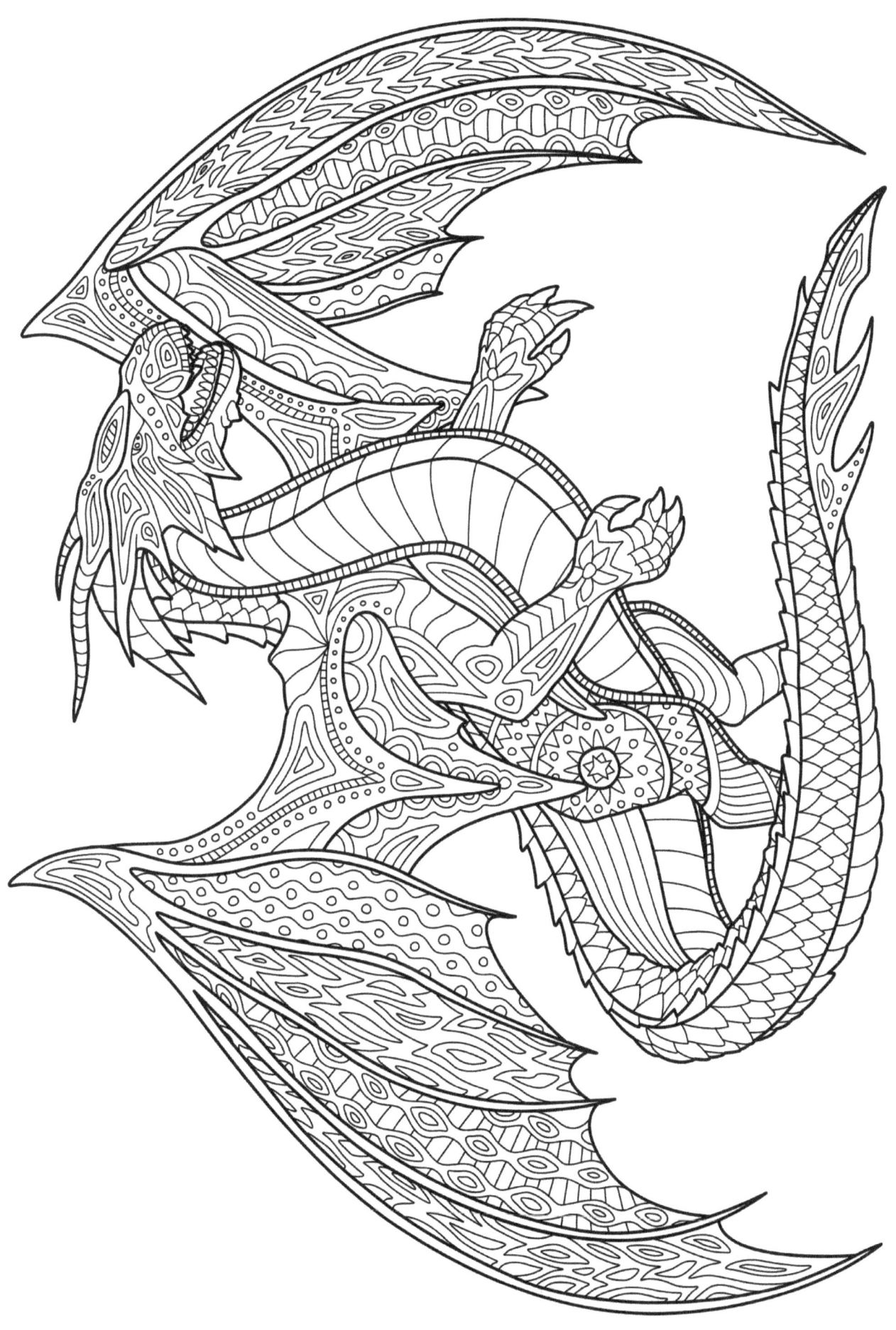

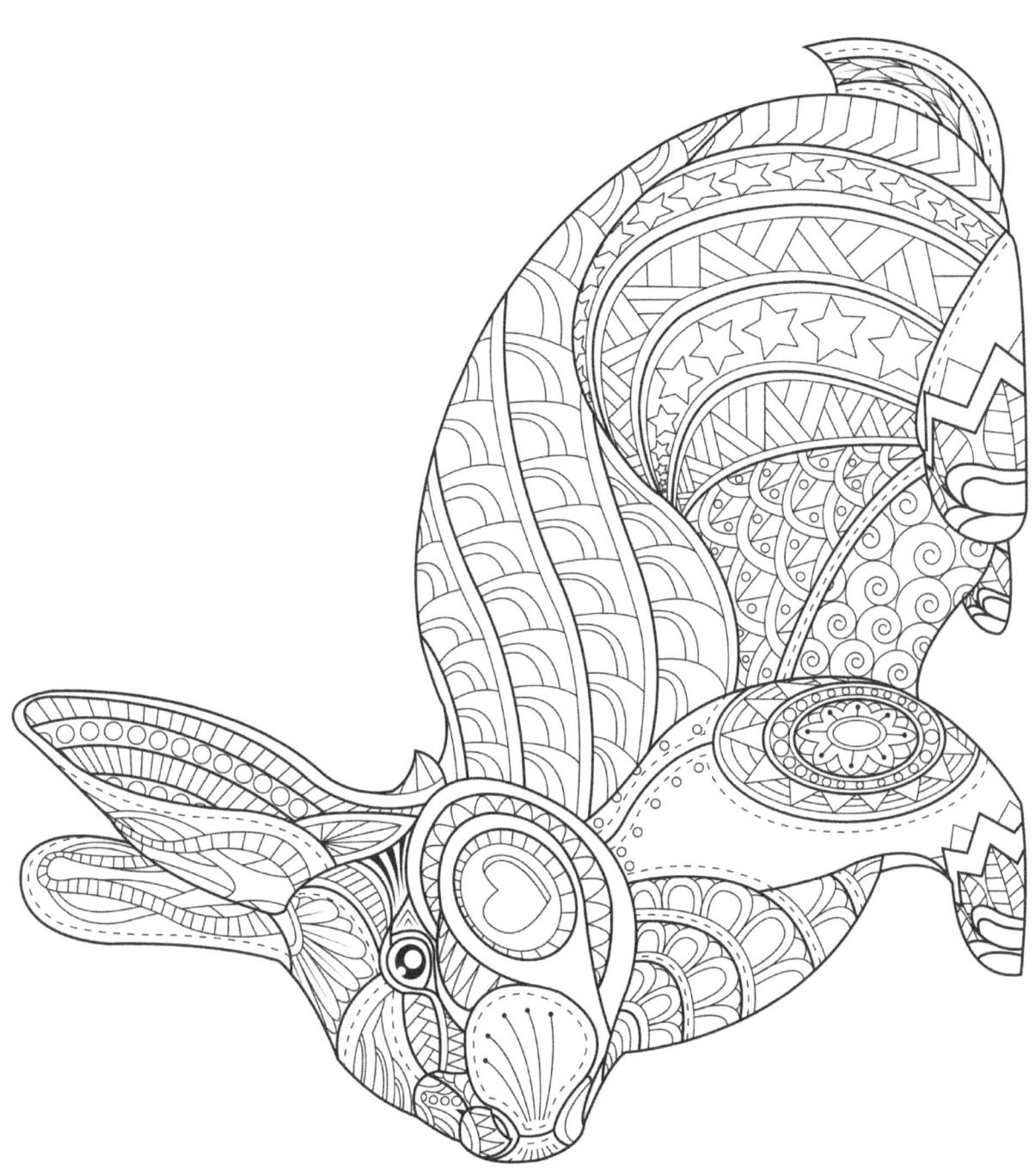

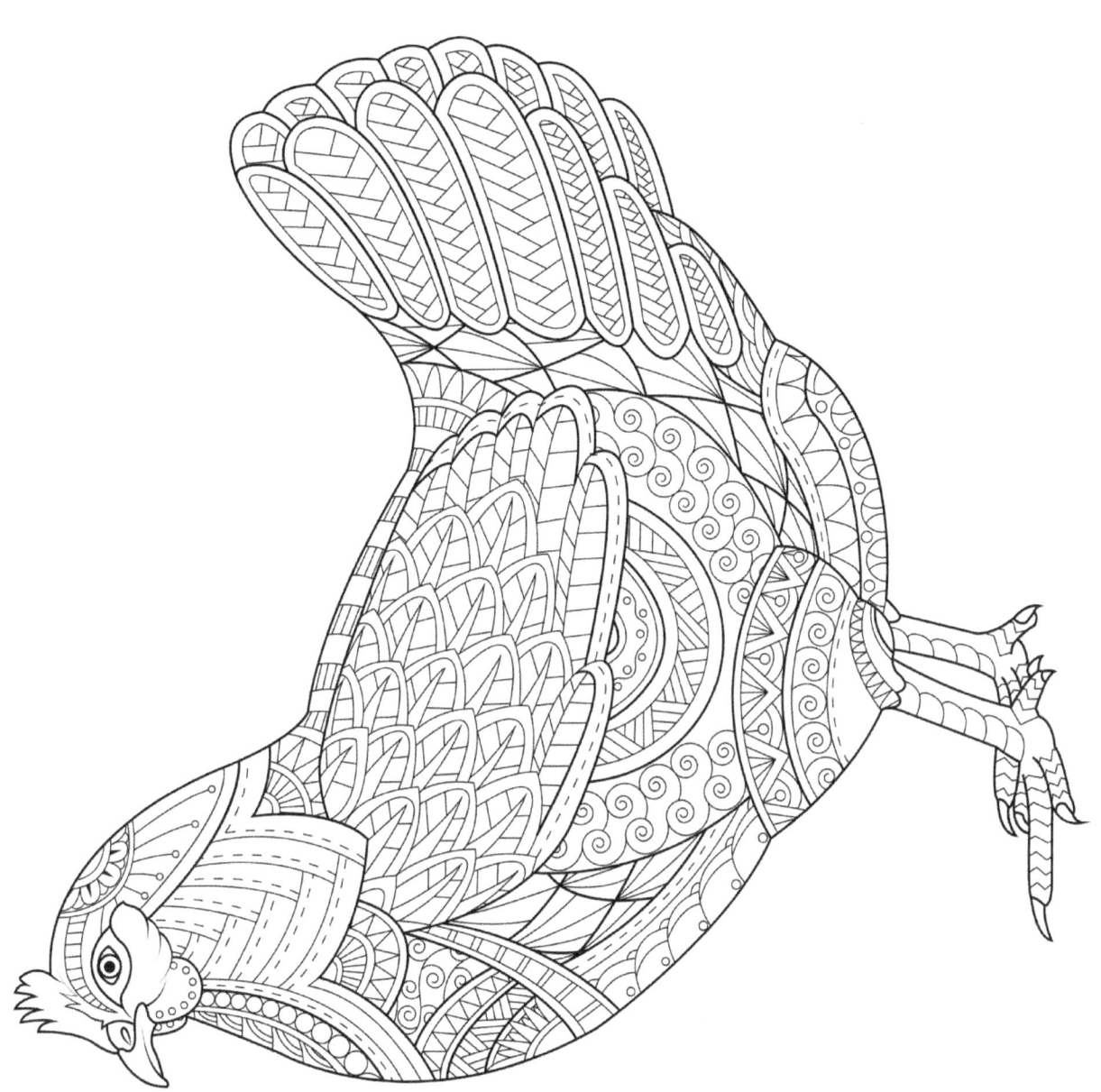

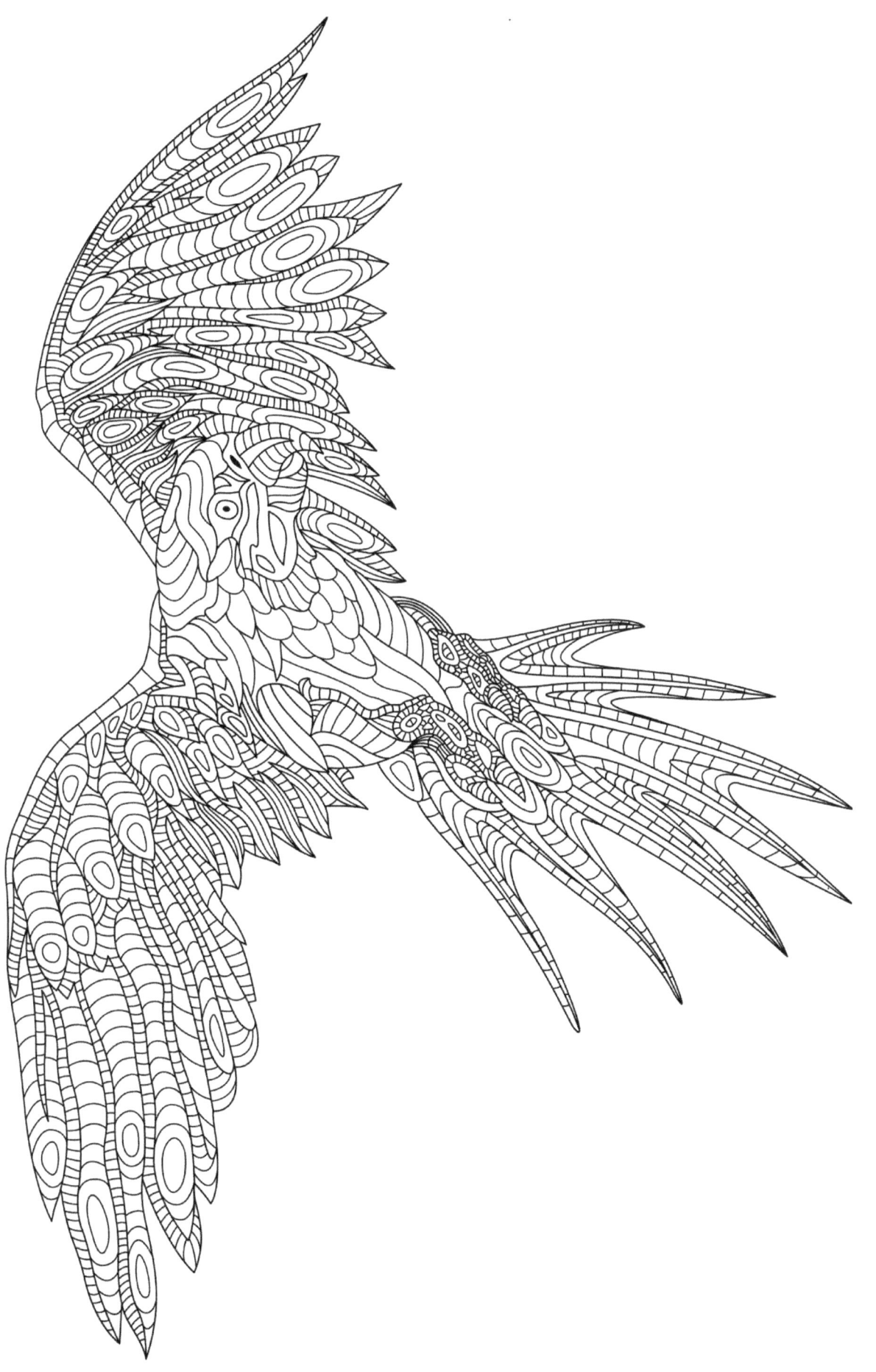

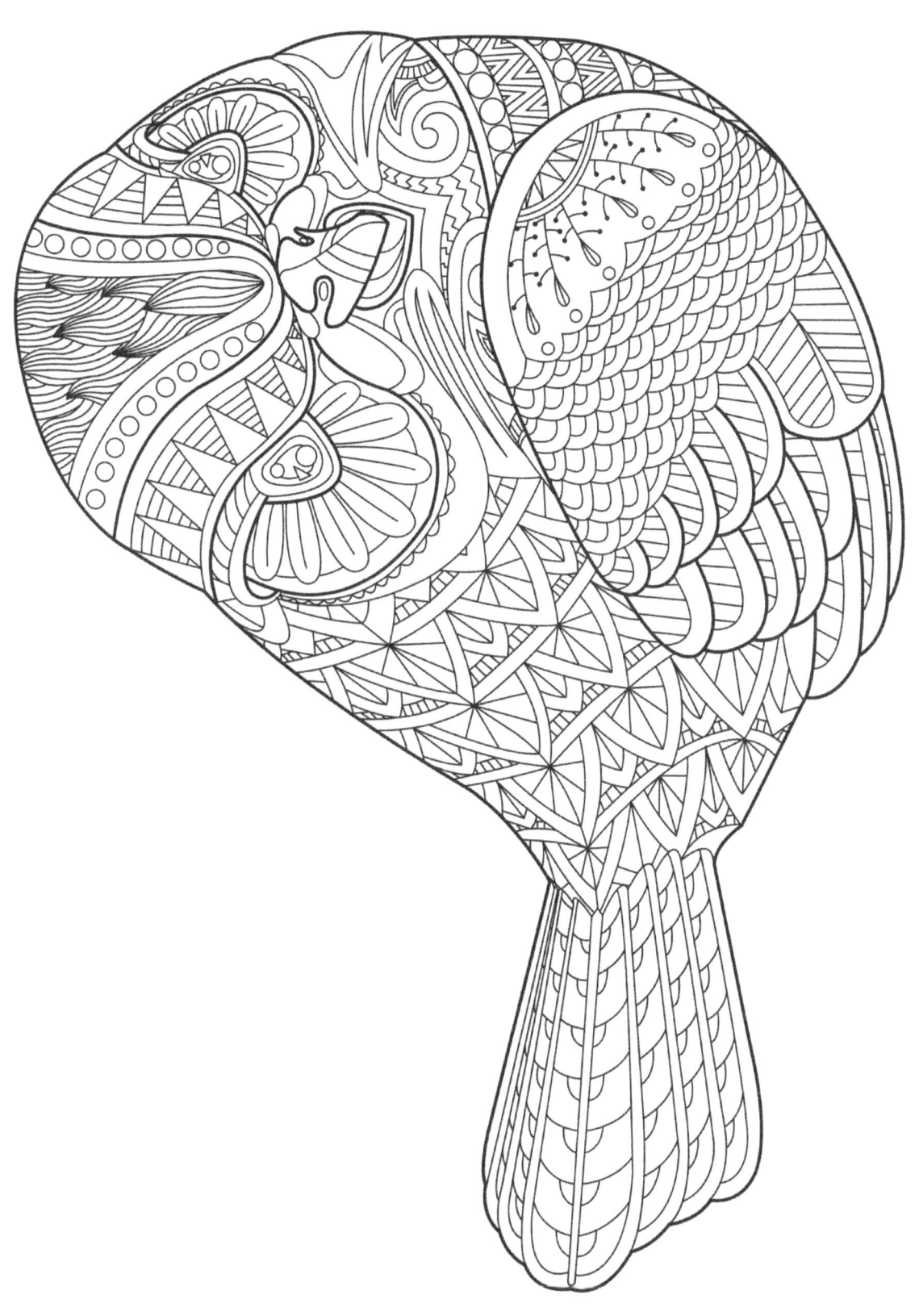

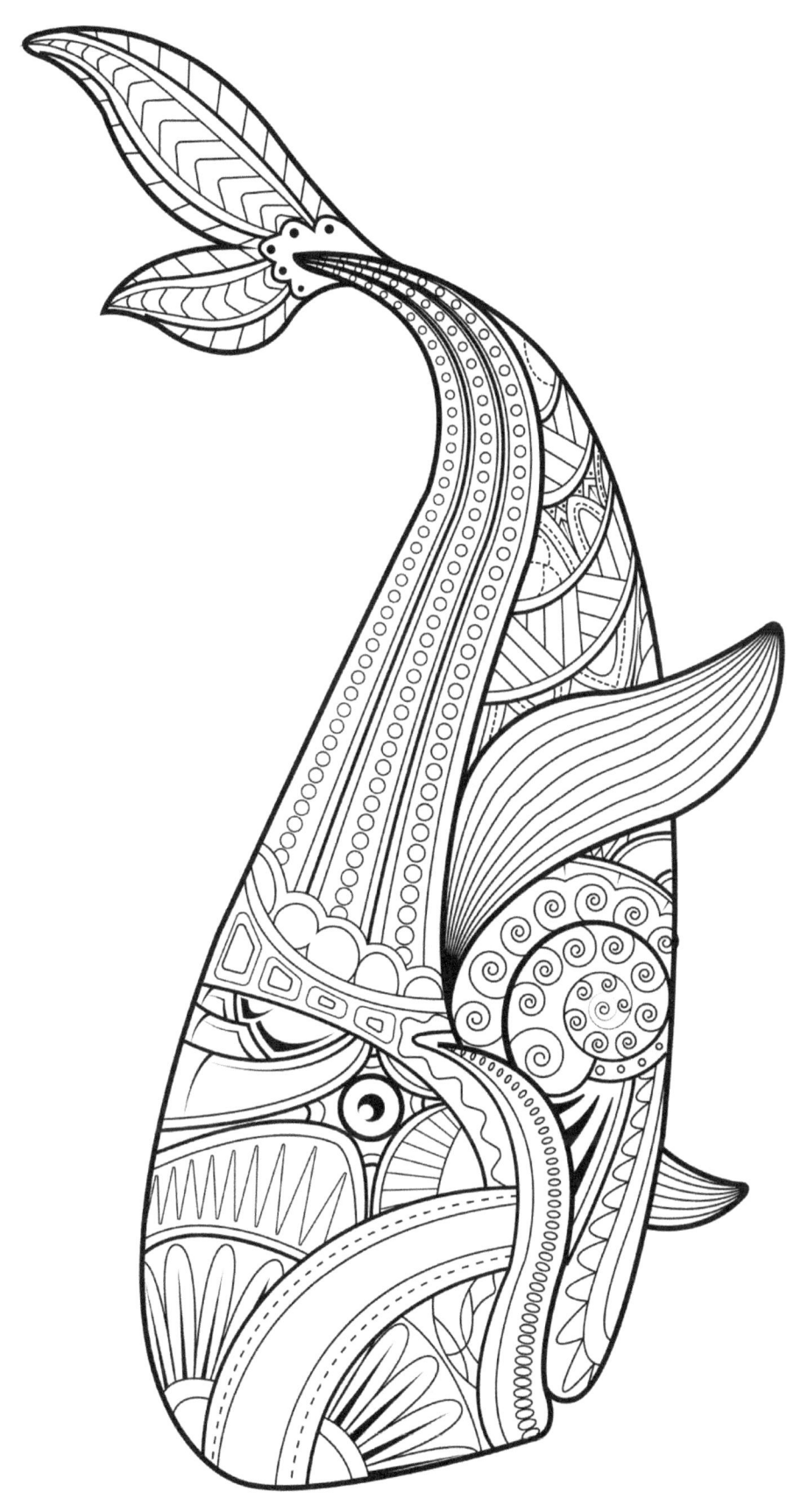

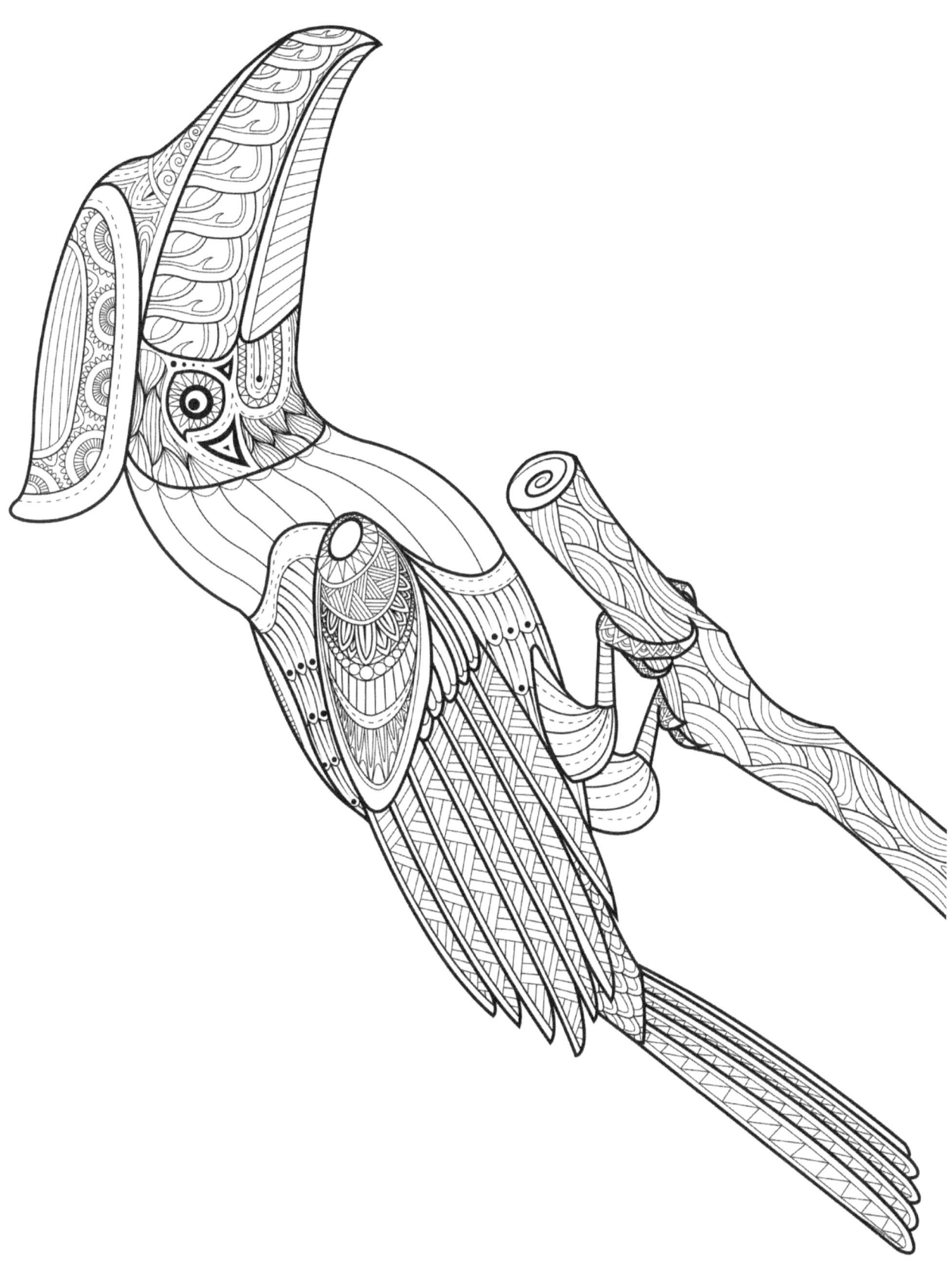

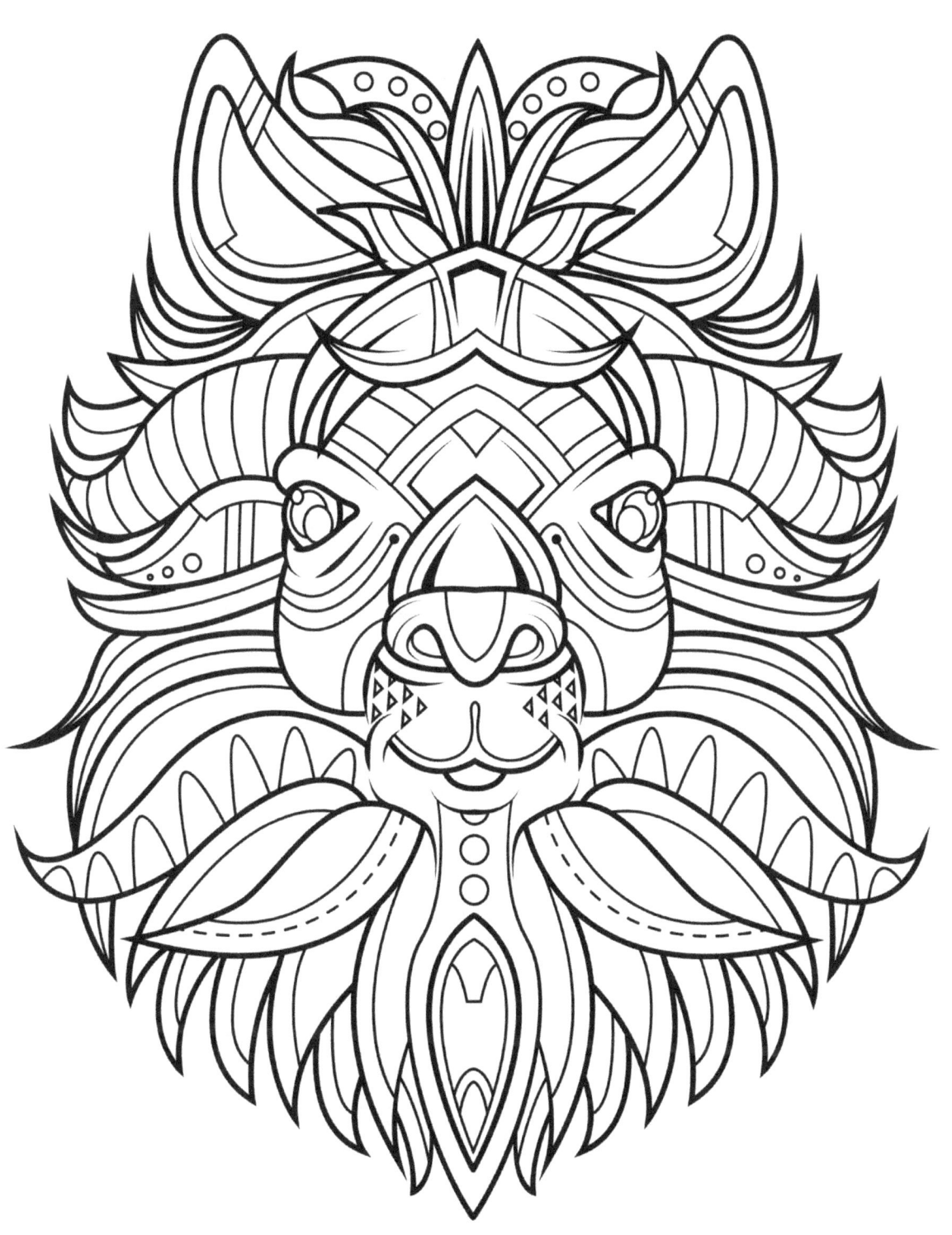

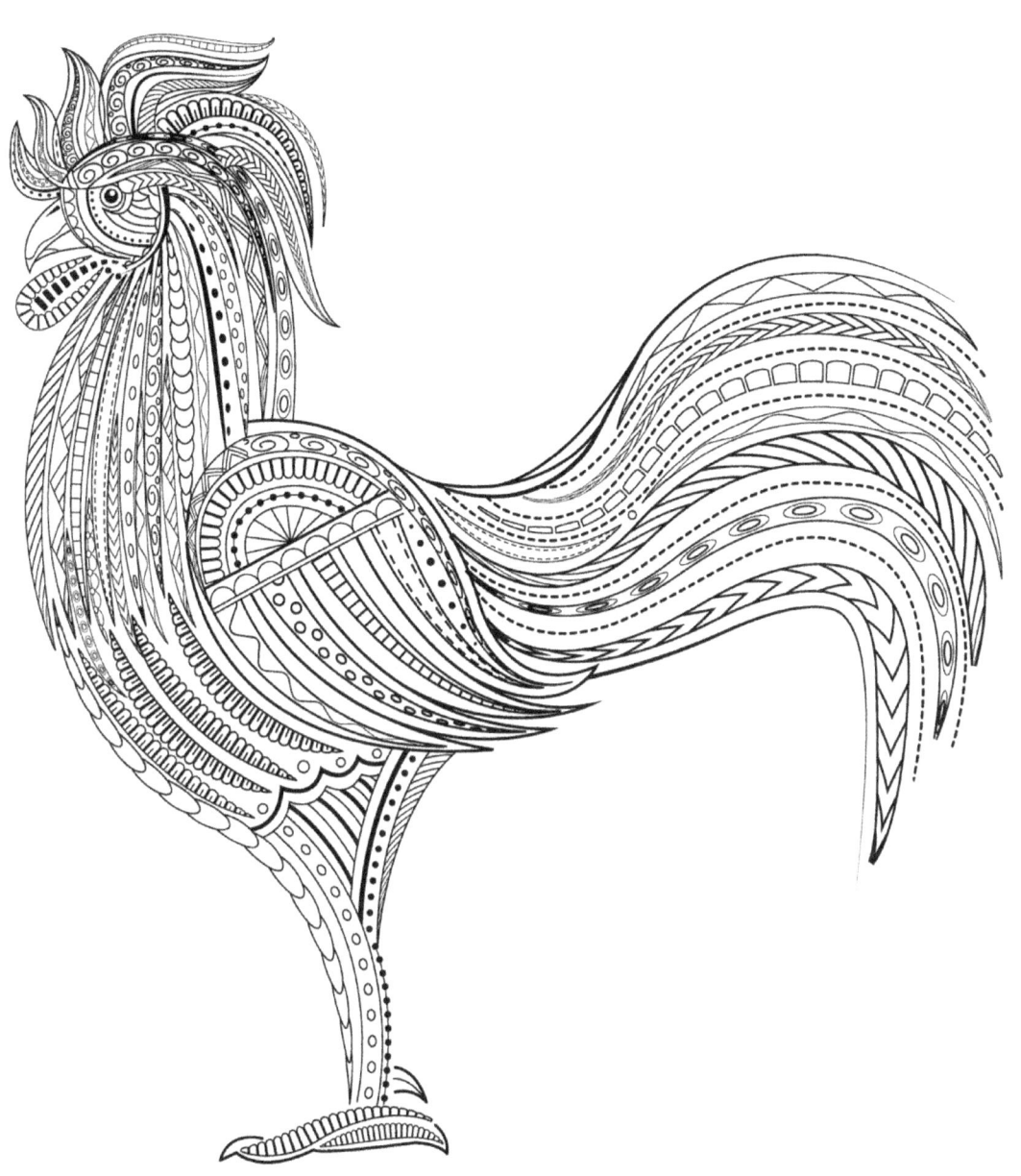

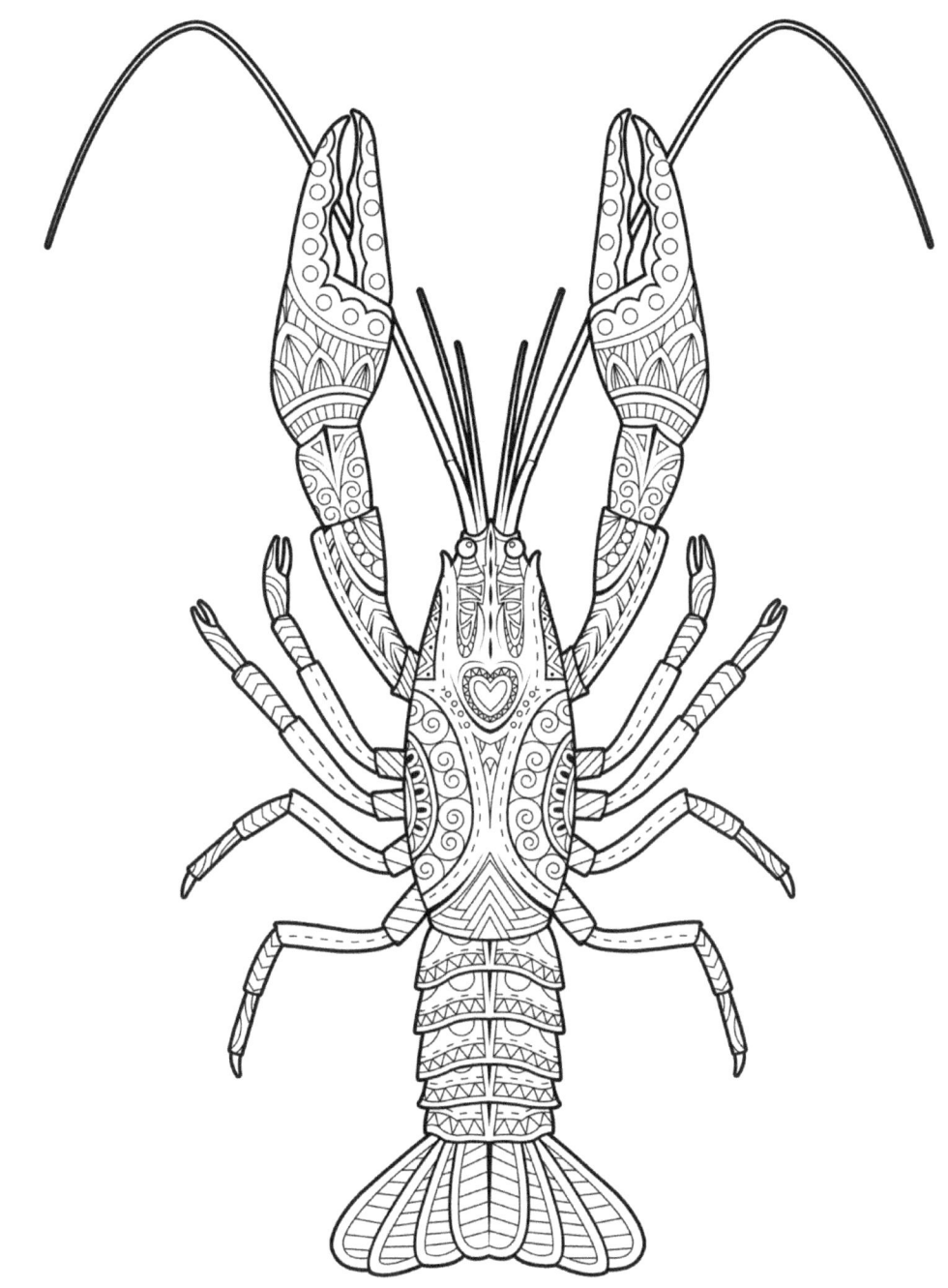

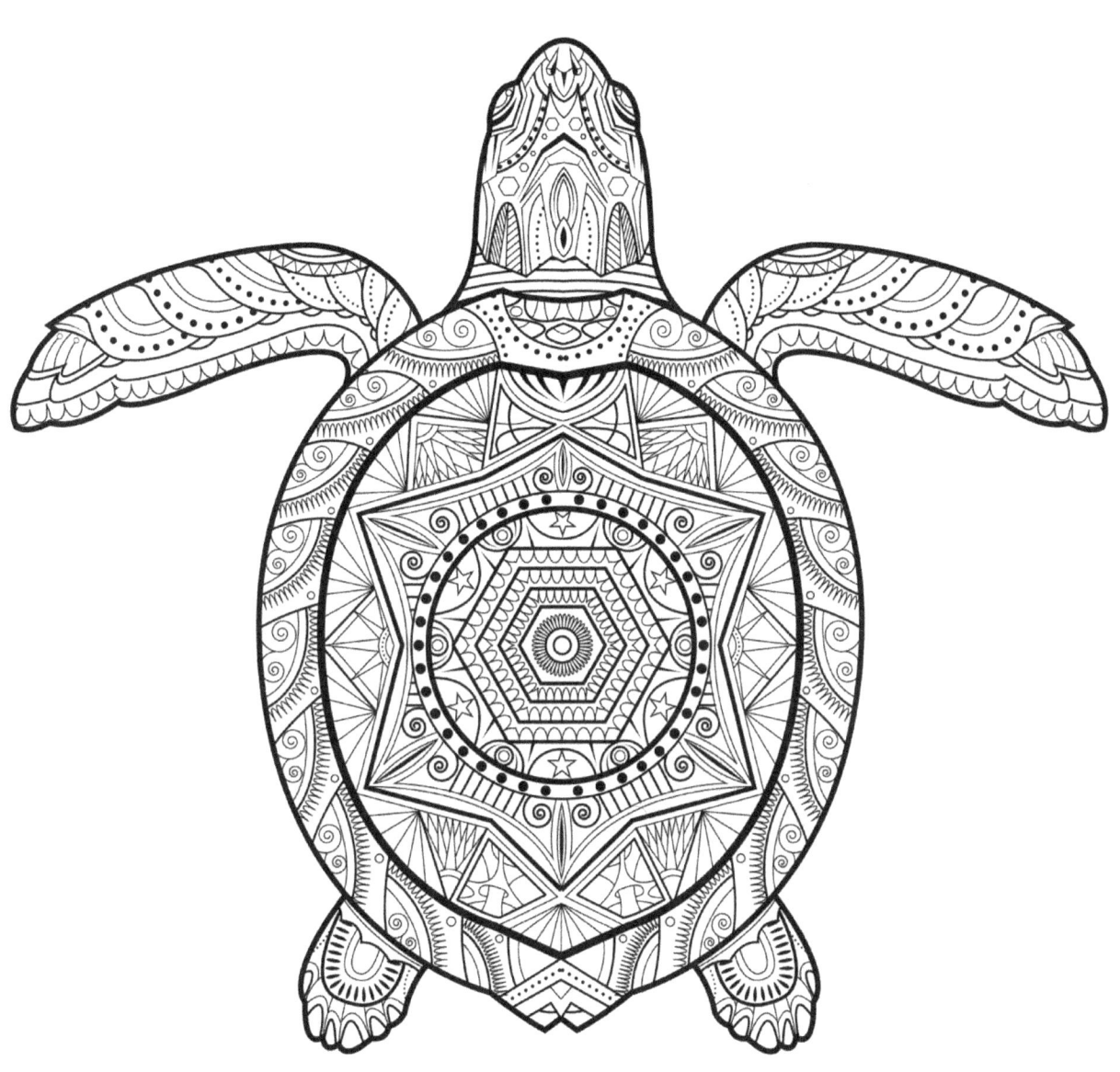

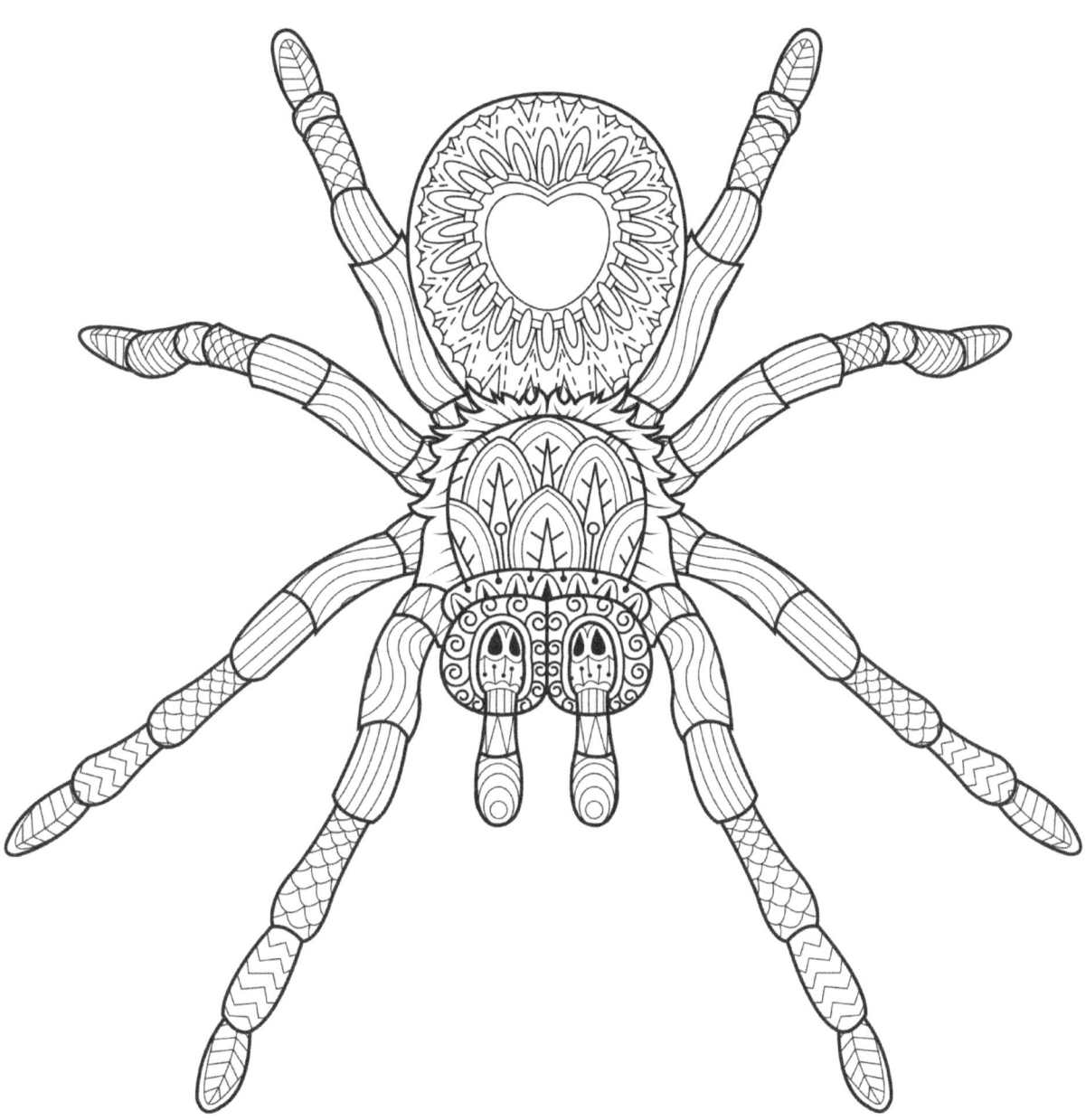

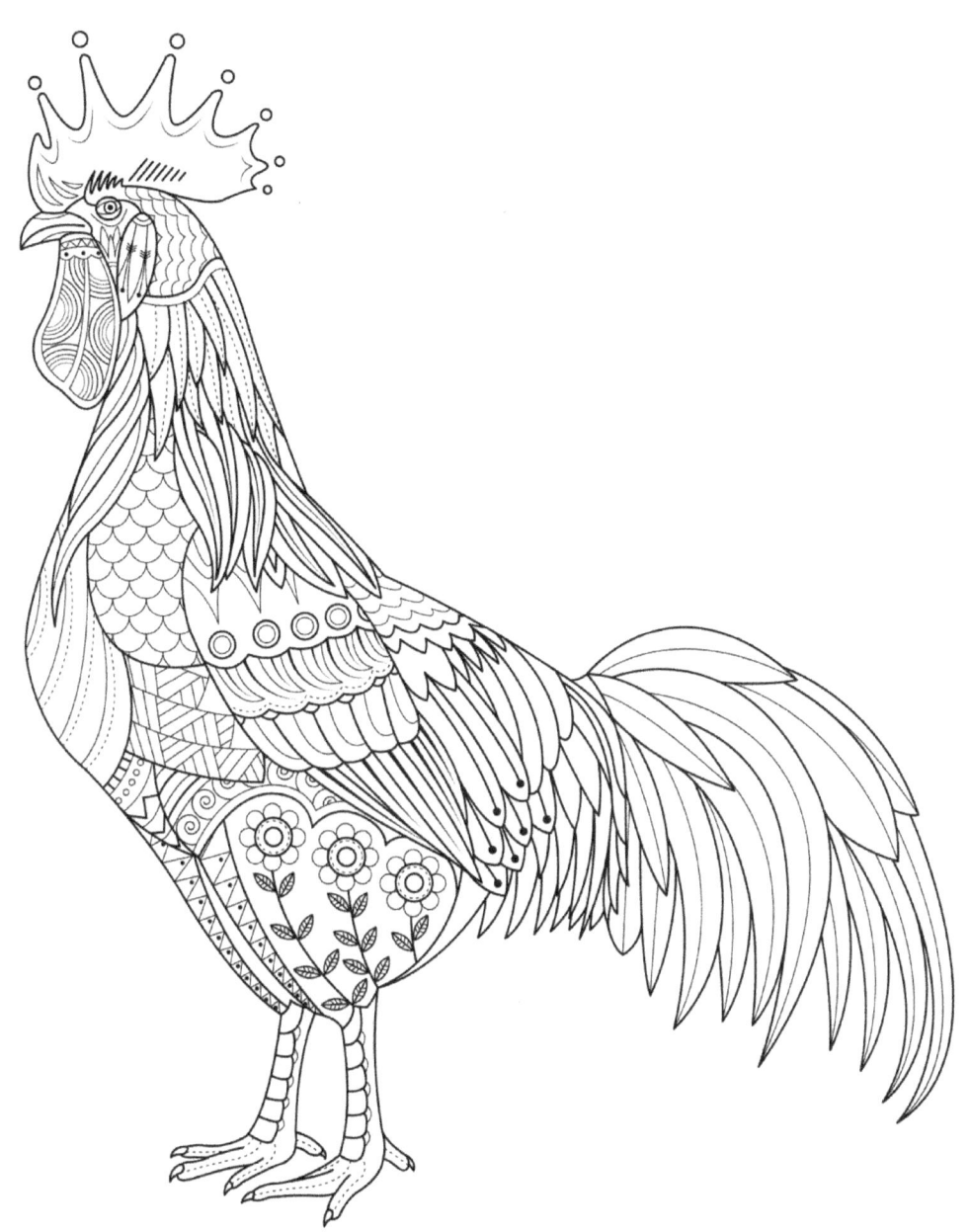

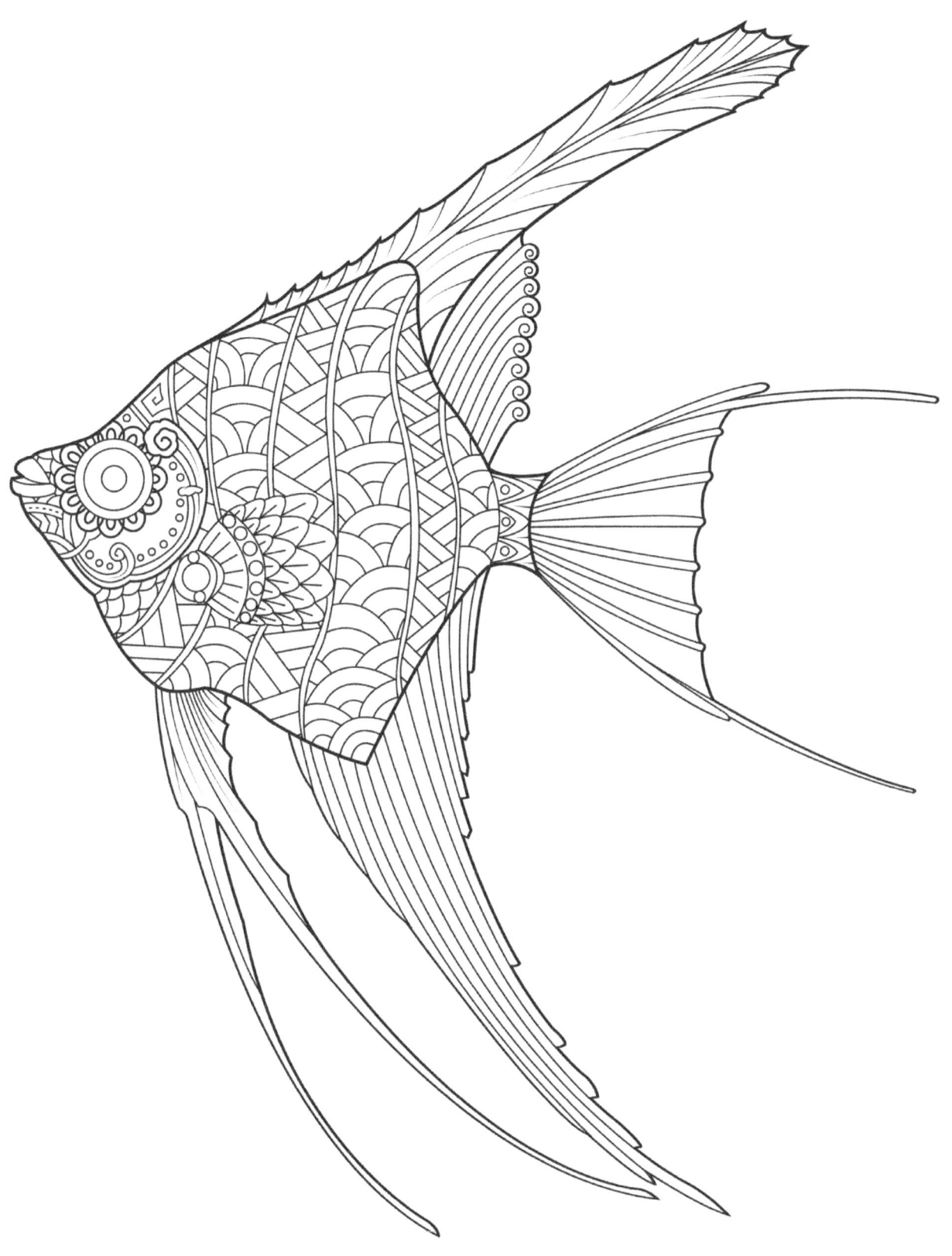

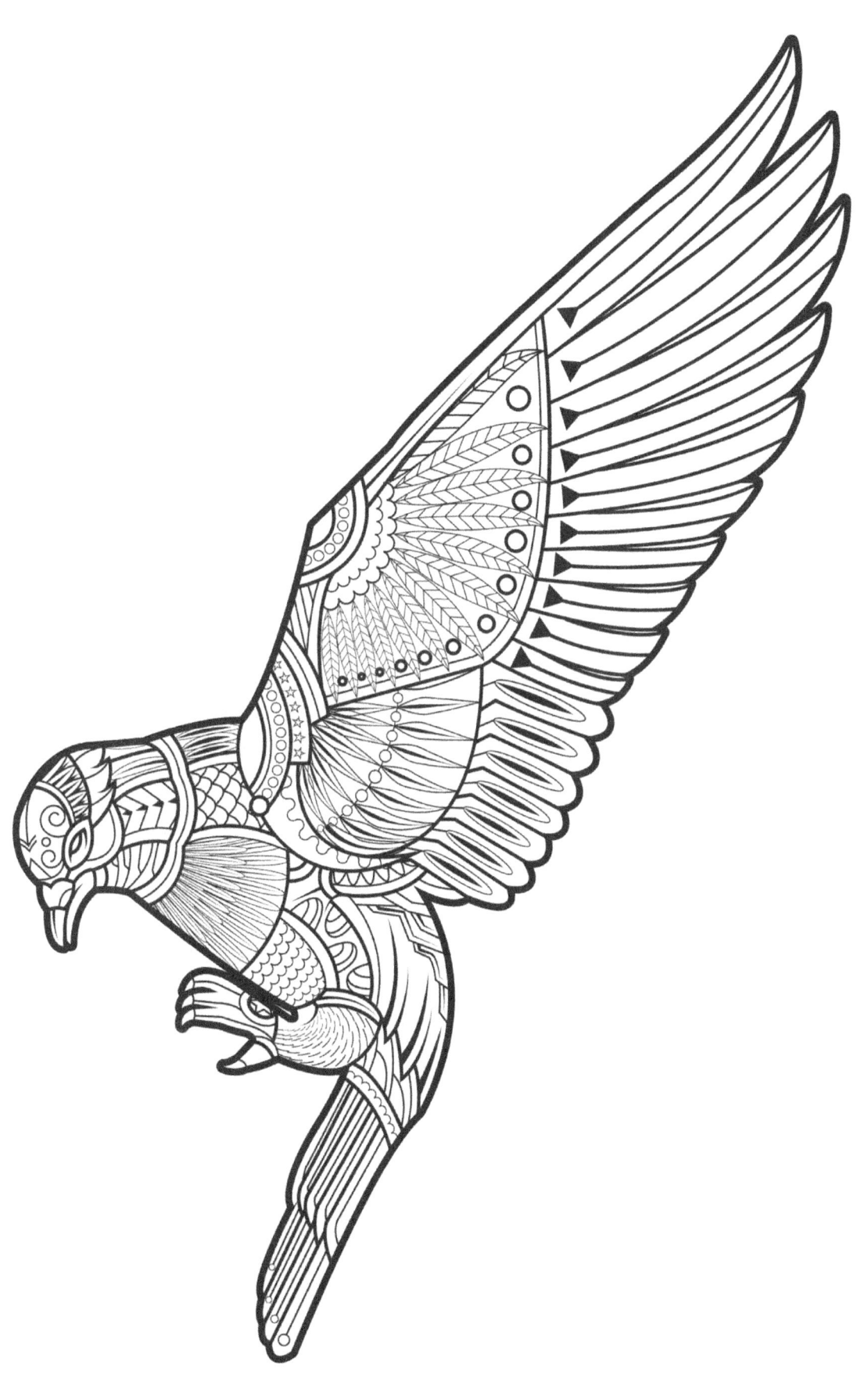

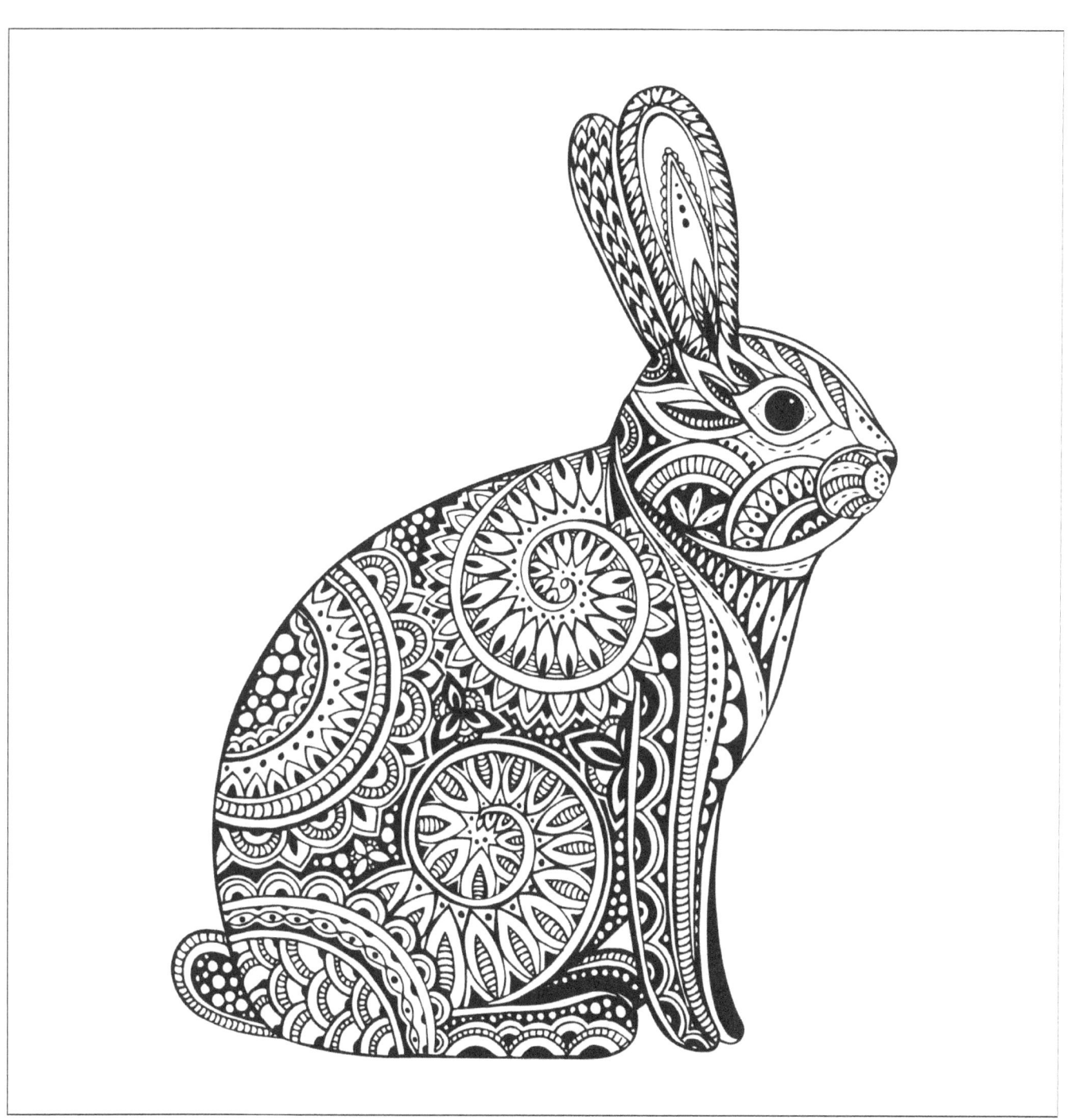

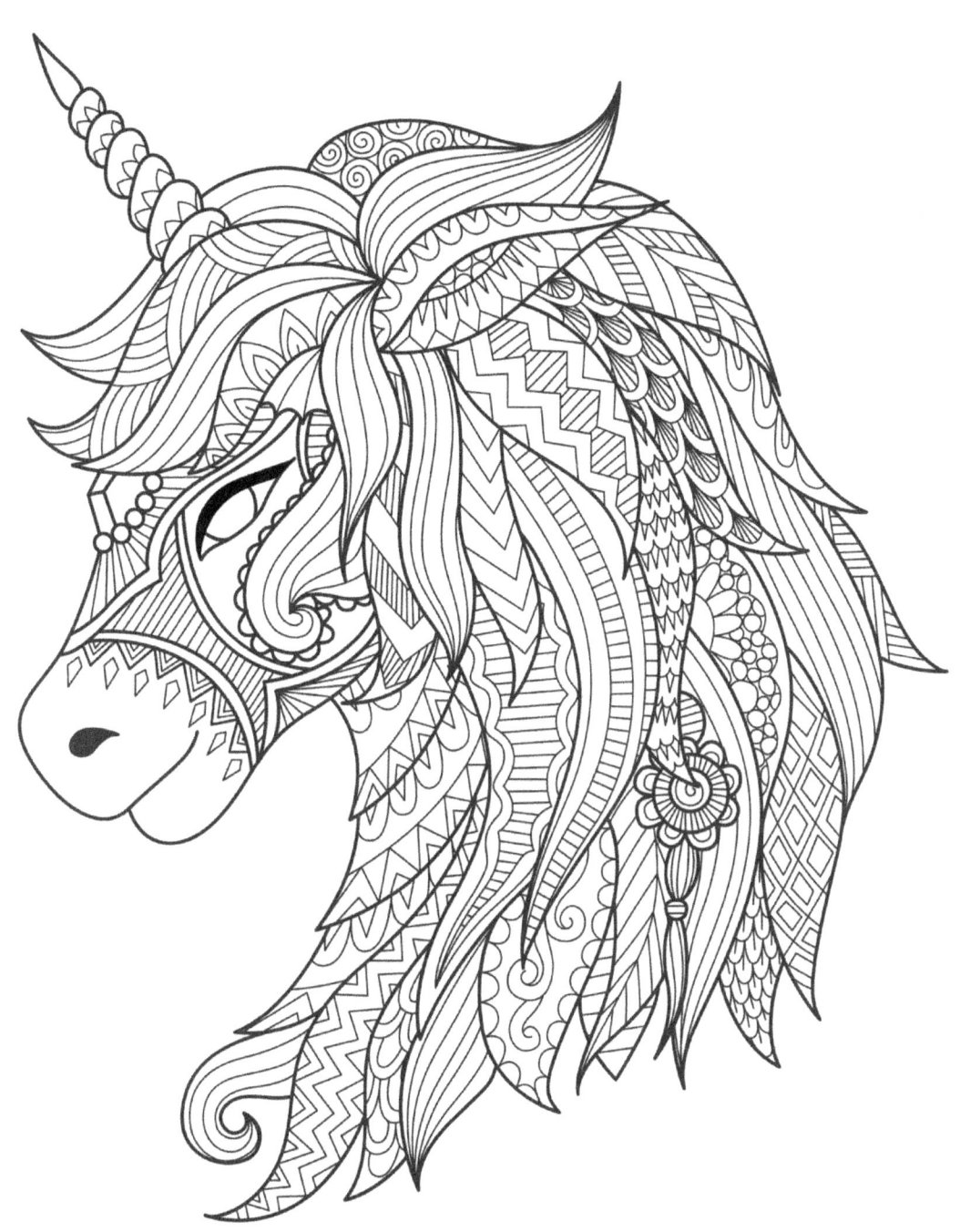

www.ingramcontent.com/pod-product-compliance
Lightning Source LLC
Chambersburg PA
CBHW081619220526
45468CB00010B/2946